# GUITAR PLAY-ALONG

## HAL•LEONARD

## Acoustic '90s

### VOL. 72

Tracking, mixing, and mastering by
Jake Johnson & Bill Maynard at Paradyme Productions
All guitars by Doug Boduch
Bass by Tom McGirr
Keyboards by Warren Wiegratz
Drums by Scott Schroedl

ISBN 978-1-4234-1444-5

Visit Hal Leonard Online at
**www.halleonard.com**

HAL•LEONARD®
CORPORATION
7777 W. BLUEMOUND RD. P.O. BOX 13819
MILWAUKEE, WISCONSIN 53213

# CONTENTS

# Guitar Notation Legend

**THE MUSICAL STAFF** shows pitches and rhythms and is divided by bar lines into measures. Pitches are named after the first seven letters of the alphabet.

**TABLATURE** graphically represents the guitar fingerboard. Each horizontal line represents a string, and each number represents a fret.

4th string, 2nd fret   1st & 2nd strings open, played together   open D chord

**HALF-STEP BEND:** Strike the note and bend up 1/2 step.

**WHOLE-STEP BEND:** Strike the note and bend up one step.

**GRACE NOTE BEND:** Strike the note and bend up as indicated. The first note does not take up any time.

**SLIGHT (MICROTONE) BEND:** Strike the note and bend up 1/4 step.

**BEND AND RELEASE:** Strike the note and bend up as indicated, then release back to the original note. Only the first note is struck.

**PRE-BEND:** Bend the note as indicated, then strike it.

**VIBRATO:** The string is vibrated by rapidly bending and releasing the note with the fretting hand.

**PALM MUTING:** The note is partially muted by the pick hand lightly touching the string(s) just before the bridge.

**HAMMER-ON:** Strike the first (lower) note with one finger, then sound the higher note (on the same string) with another finger by fretting it without picking.

**PULL-OFF:** Place both fingers on the notes to be sounded. Strike the first note and without picking, pull the finger off to sound the second (lower) note.

**LEGATO SLIDE:** Strike the first note and then slide the same fret-hand finger up or down to the second note. The second note is not struck.

**SHIFT SLIDE:** Same as legato slide, except the second note is struck.

**TRILL:** Very rapidly alternate between the notes indicated by continuously hammering on and pulling off.

**TAPPING:** Hammer ("tap") the fret indicated with the pick-hand index or middle finger and pull off to the note fretted by the fret hand.

**NATURAL HARMONIC:** Strike the note while the fret-hand lightly touches the string directly over the fret indicated.

**PINCH HARMONIC:** The note is fretted normally and a harmonic is produced by adding the edge of the thumb or the tip of the index finger of the pick hand to the normal pick attack.

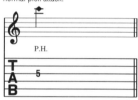

**TREMOLO PICKING:** The note is picked as rapidly and continuously as possible.

**VIBRATO BAR DIVE AND RETURN:** The pitch of the note or chord is dropped a specified number of steps (in rhythm) then returned to the original pitch.

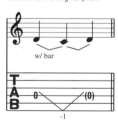

**VIBRATO BAR SCOOP:** Depress the bar just before striking the note, then quickly release the bar.

**VIBRATO BAR DIP:** Strike the note and then immediately drop a specified number of steps, then release back to the original pitch.

# Additional Musical Definitions

 *(accent)* • Accentuate note (play it louder)

*(staccato)* • Play the note short

***D.S. al Coda*** • Go back to the sign (𝄋), then play until the measure marked ***"To Coda"***, then skip to the section labelled ***"Coda."***

***D.C. al Fine*** • Go back to the beginning of the song and play until the measure marked ***"Fine"*** (end).

**Fill** • Label used to identify a brief melodic figure which is to be inserted into the arrangement.

**N.C.** • No Chord

• Repeat measures between signs.

• When a repeated section has different endings, play the first ending only the first time and the second ending only the second time.

5

# All Apologies

**Words and Music by Kurt Cobain**

Drop D tuning, down 1/2 step:
(low to high) D♭-A♭-D♭-G♭-B♭-E♭

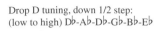

**Intro**
**Moderately** ♩ = 109

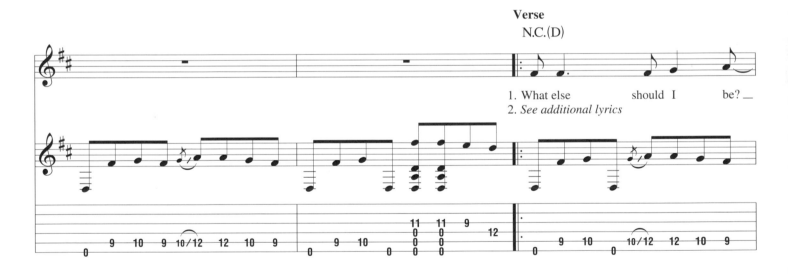

1. What else should I be? __
2. *See additional lyrics*

__ All a - pol - o - gies. __

bur - ied. ___      Mar - ried, ___

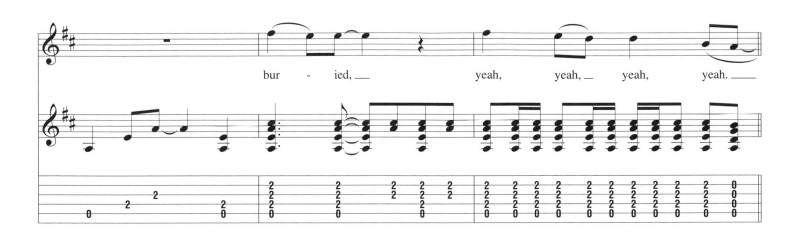

bur - ied, ___      yeah,    yeah, ___ yeah,     yeah. ___

**Outro**

N.C.(D)

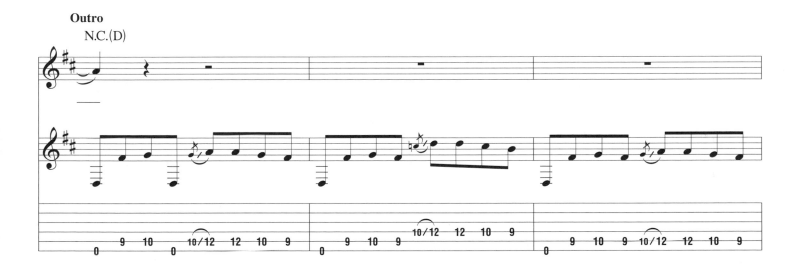

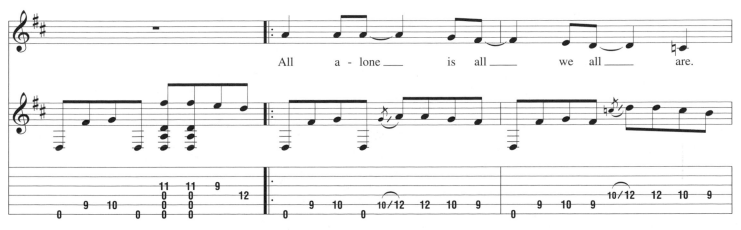

All   a - lone ___ is all ___ we all ___ are.

9

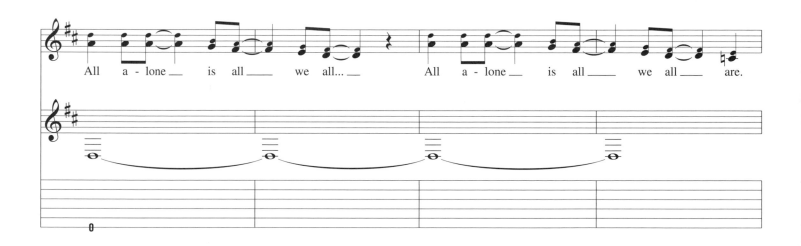

Gtr. tacet

All a - lone ____ is all _____ we all _____ are.

*Additional Lyrics*

2. I wish I was like you: easily amused.
   Find my nest of salt; ev'rything is my fault.
   I'll take all the blame; aqua seafoam shame.
   Sunburn with freezer burn;
   Choking on the ashes of her enemy.

# Disarm

**Words and Music by Billy Corgan**

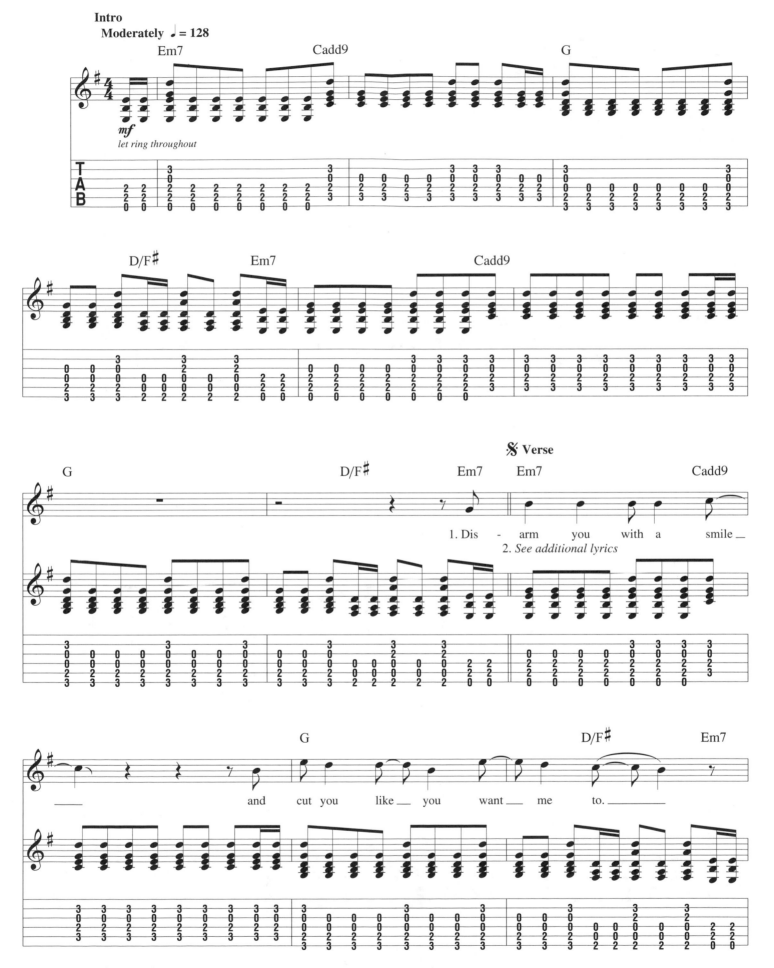

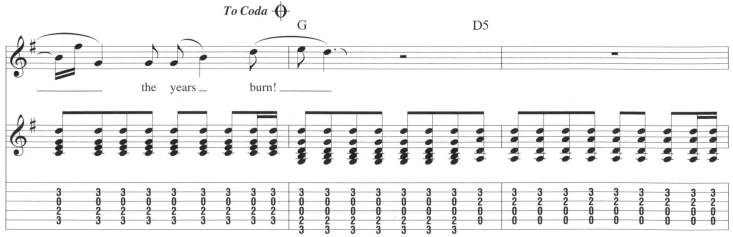

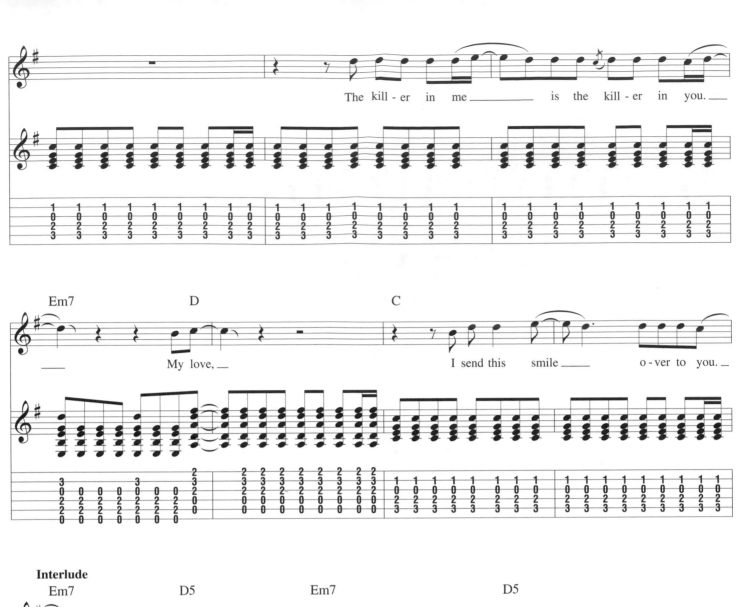

The kill - er in me _____ is the kill - er in you. _____

Em7　　　　　D　　　　　　　　C

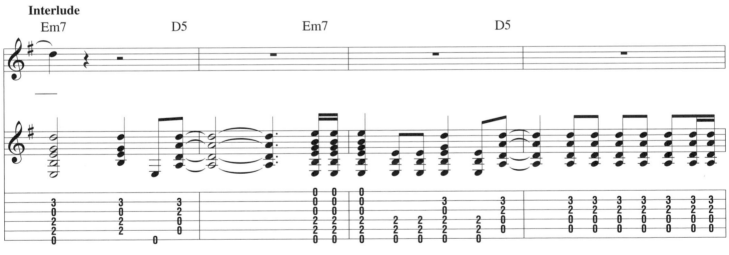

_____ My love, ___　　　I send this smile _____ o - ver to you. ___

**Interlude**

Em7　　　　　D5　　　　　Em7　　　　　D5

**D.S. al Coda**

C

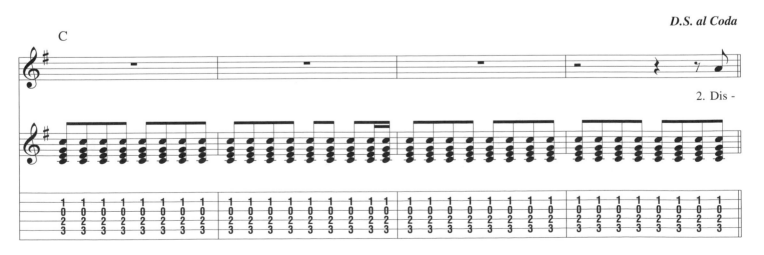

2. Dis -

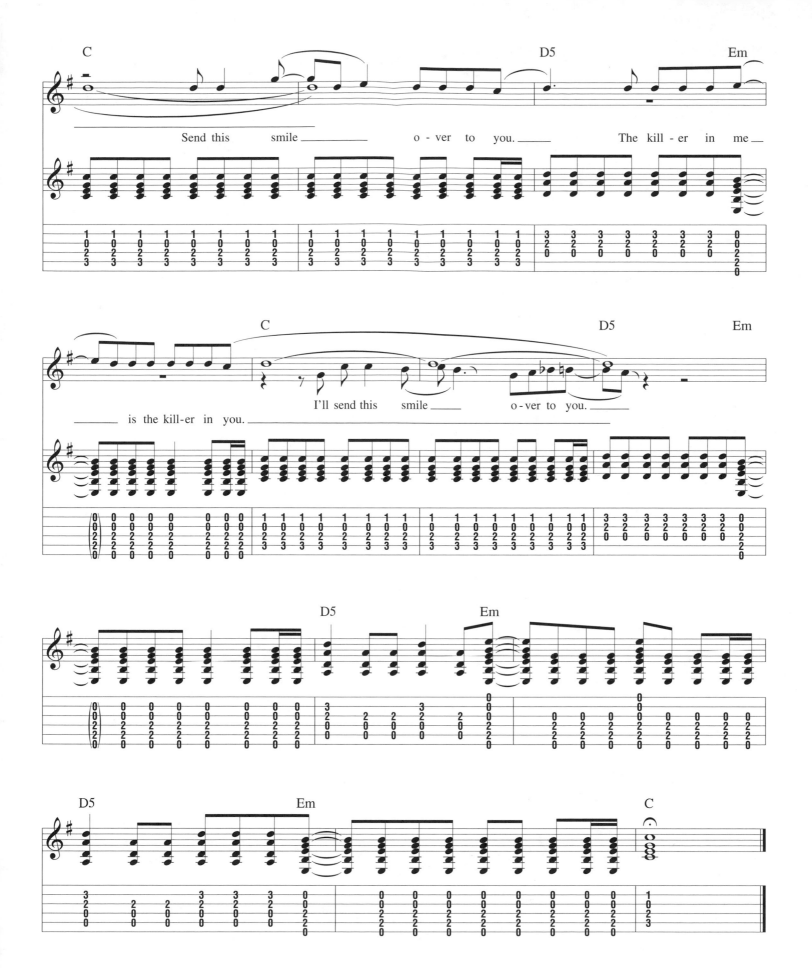

*Additional Lyrics*

2. Disarm you with a smile
   And leave you like they left me here
   To wither in denial.
   The bitterness of one who's left alone.
   Oo, the years burn.
   Oo, the years burn.

# Daughter

**Words and Music by Stone Gossard, Jeffrey Ament, Eddie Vedder, Michael McCready and David Abbruzzese**

**Pre-Chorus**

**Chorus**

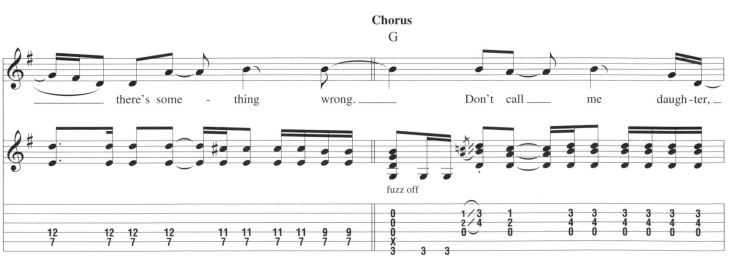

**Interlude**

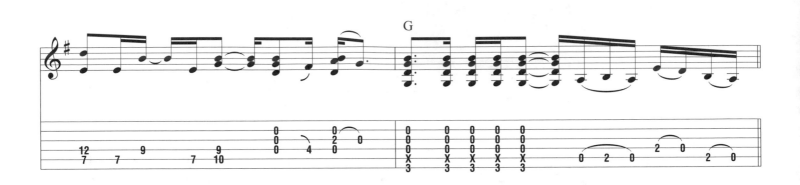

**Bridge**

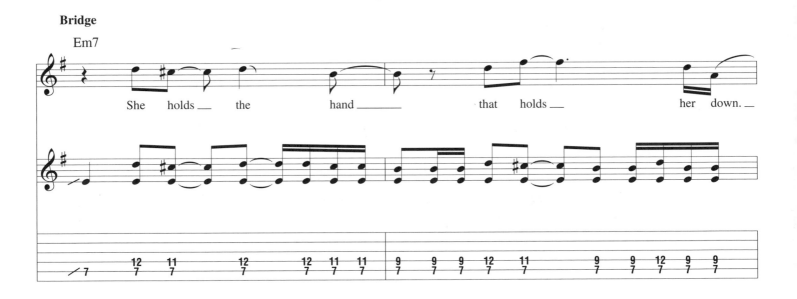

**Guitar Solo**

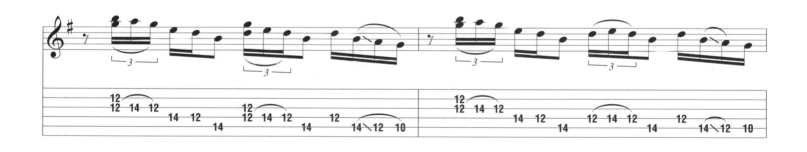

**Chorus**

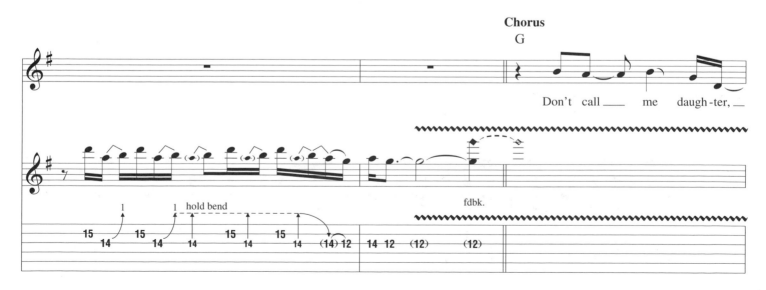

Don't call ___ me daugh-ter, ___

23

**Interlude**

Em7

**Outro**

Em7

The shades ____ go ____ down. ____

The shades ____ go ____ down. ____

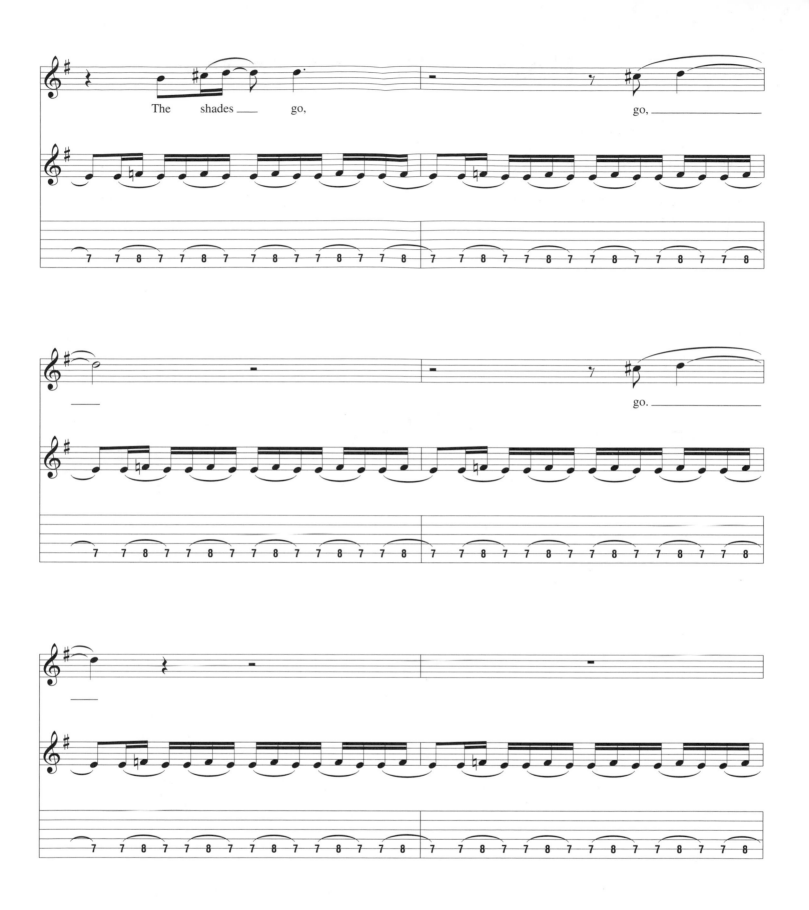

*Play 4 times and fade*

# Heaven Beside You

**Lyrics by Jerry Cantrell**

**Music by Jerry Cantrell and Mike Inez**

Tune down 1/2 step:
(low to high) E♭-A♭-D♭-G♭-B♭-E♭

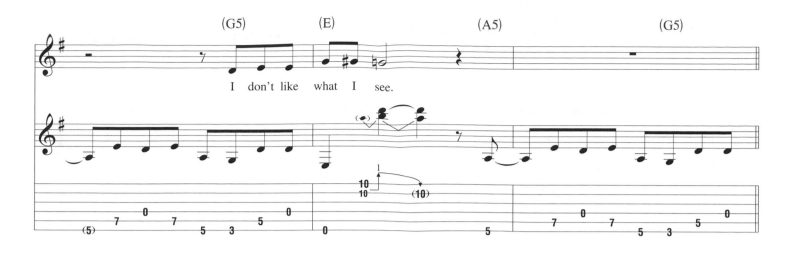

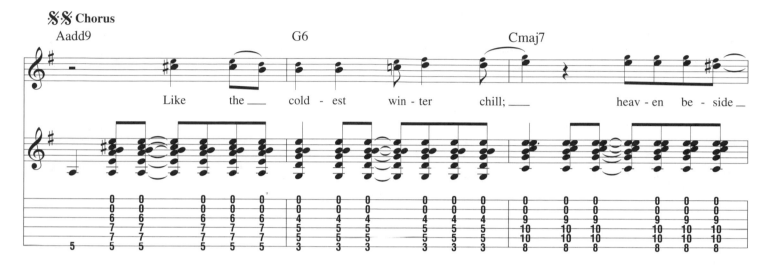

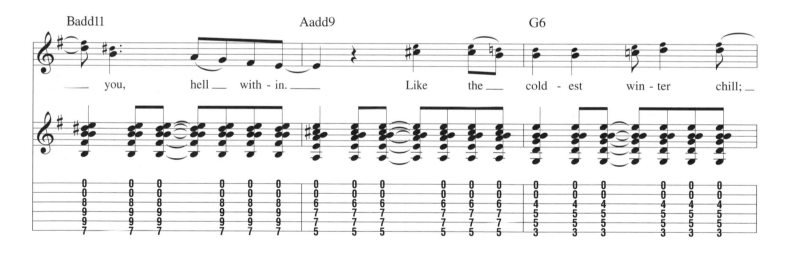

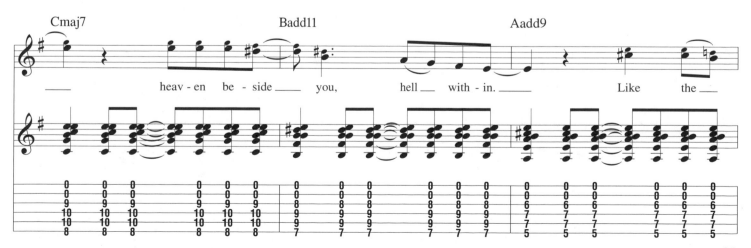

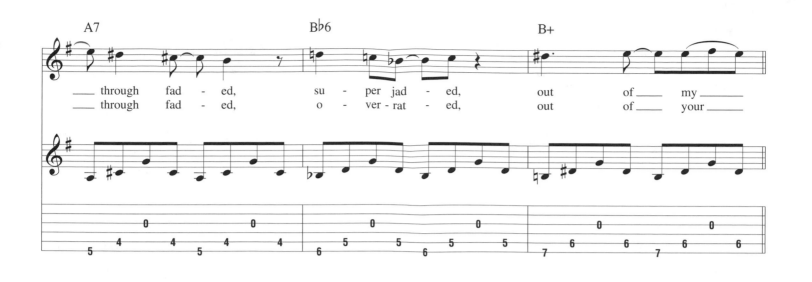

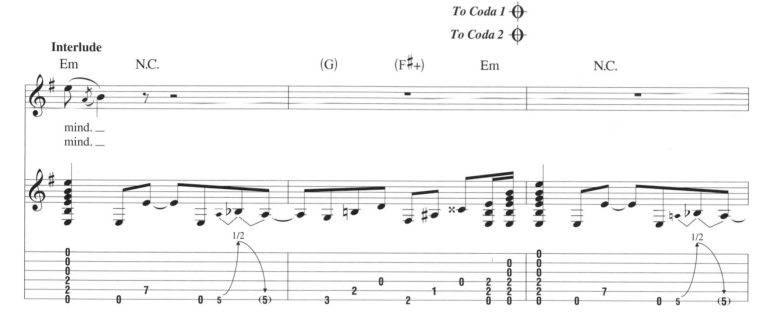

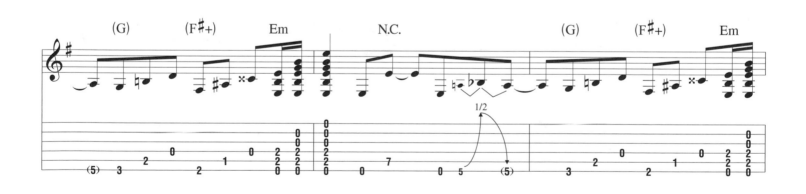

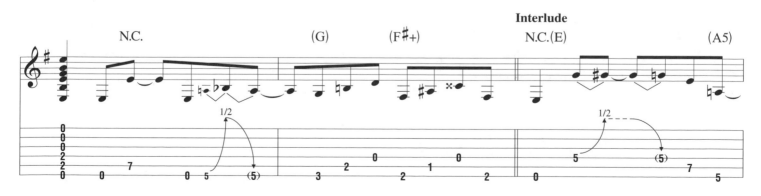

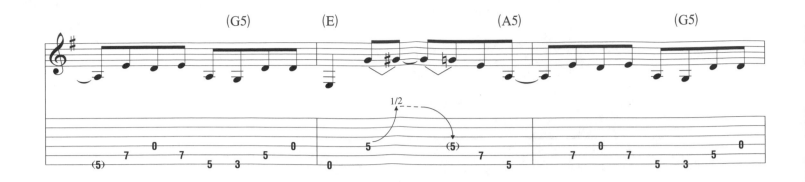

*D.S. al Coda 1*

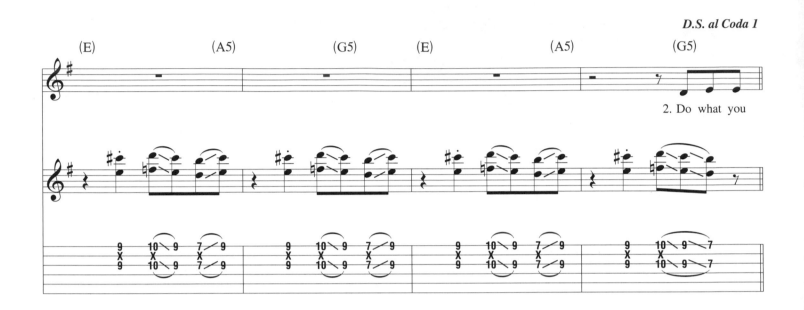

2. Do what you

## ✦ Coda 1

**Guitar Solo**

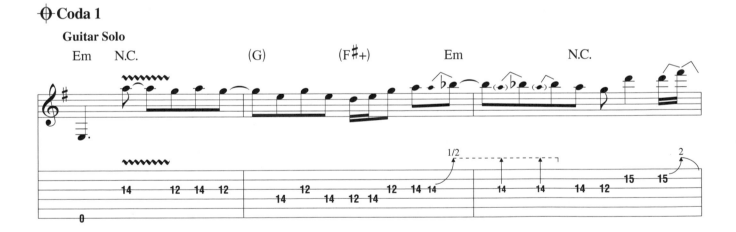

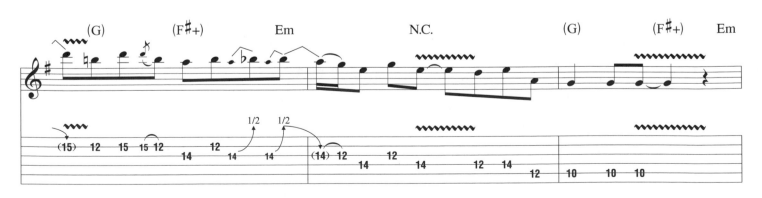

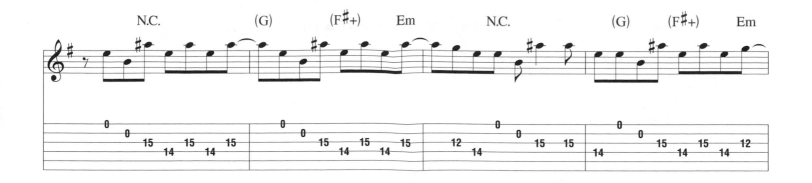

*D.S.S. al Coda 2*

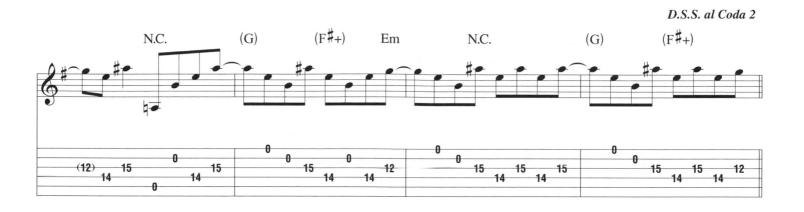

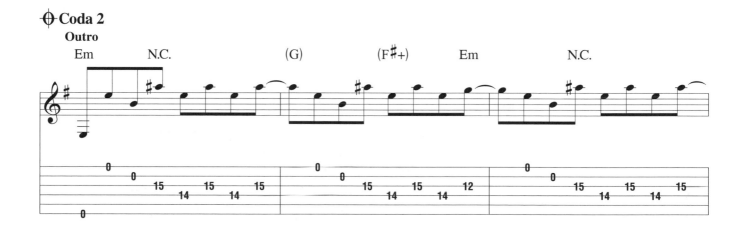

⊕ **Coda 2**

**Outro**

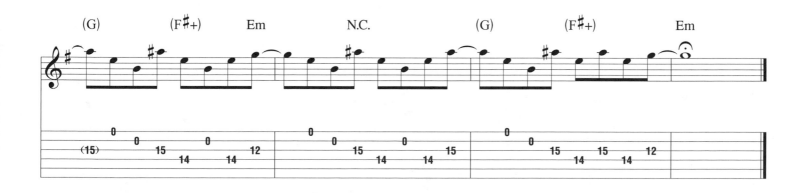

*Additional Lyrics*

2. Do what you wanna do.
Go out and seek your truth.
When I'm down and blue,
Rather be me than you.

# My Friends

### Words and Music by Anthony Kiedis, Flea, Chad Smith and David Navarro

Drop D tuning:
(low to high) D-A-D-G-B-E

**Intro**

**Moderately** ♩ = 84

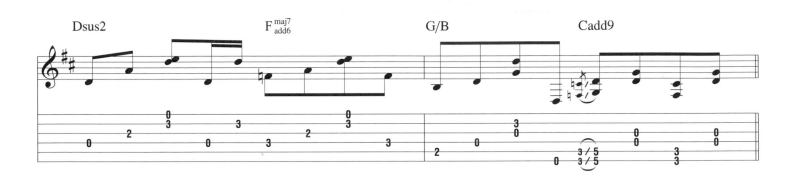

**Verse**

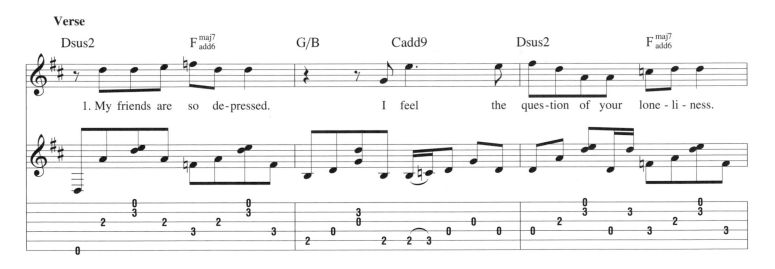

1. My friends are so de-pressed. I feel the ques-tion of your lone-li-ness.

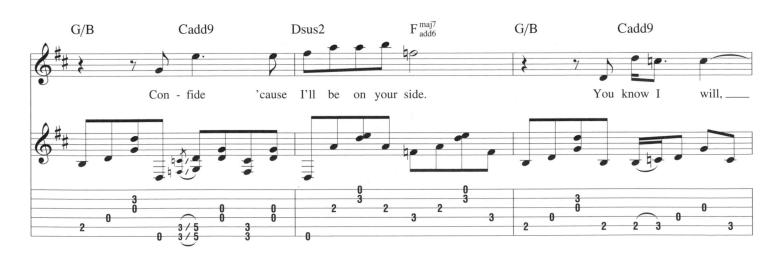

Con-fide 'cause I'll be on your side. You know I will,___

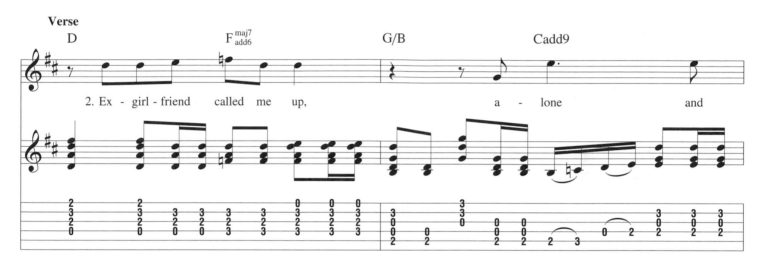

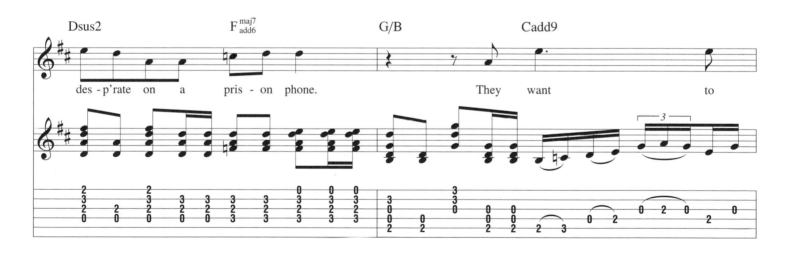

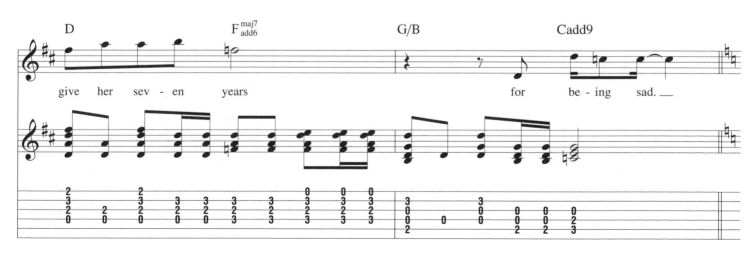

**Chorus**

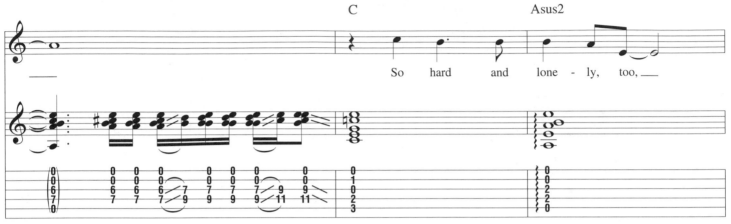

**Verse**

*2nd time, dist. off

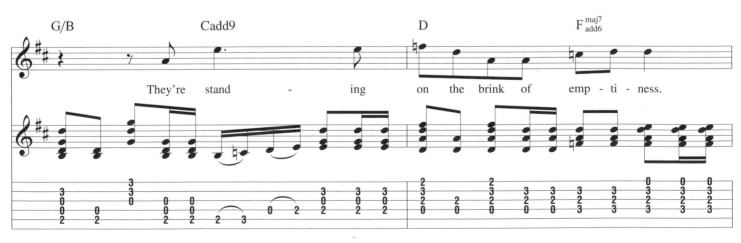

36

No words, I know what to ex - press,

*To Coda* ⊕
**Chorus**

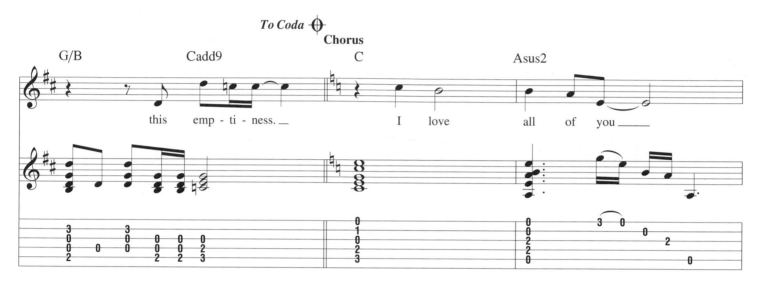

this emp - ti - ness. ___ I love all of you ___

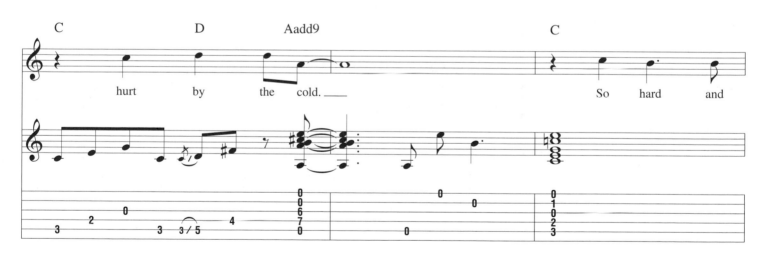

hurt by the cold. ___ So hard and

lone - ly, too, ___ when you don't know ___ your - self. ___

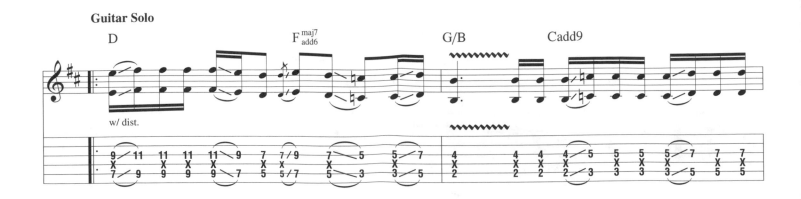

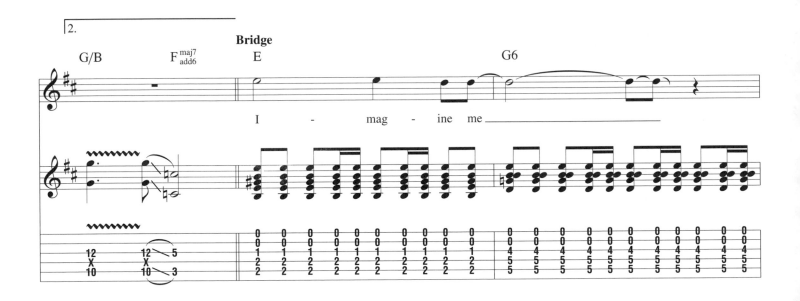

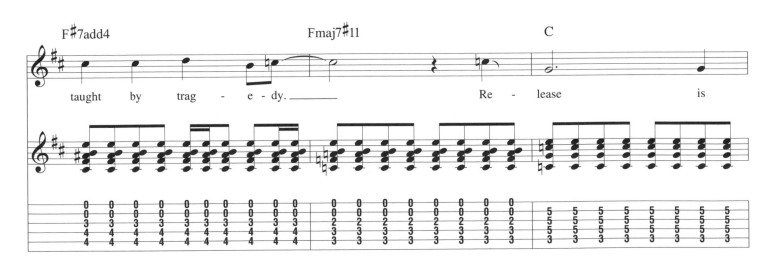

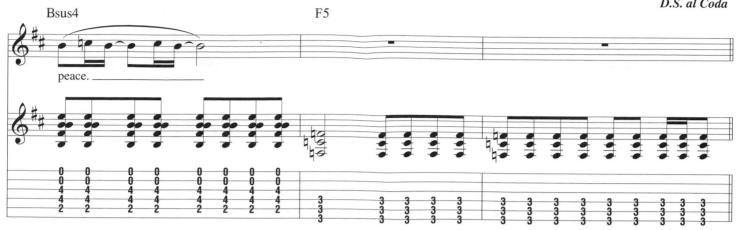

**Coda**

**Chorus**

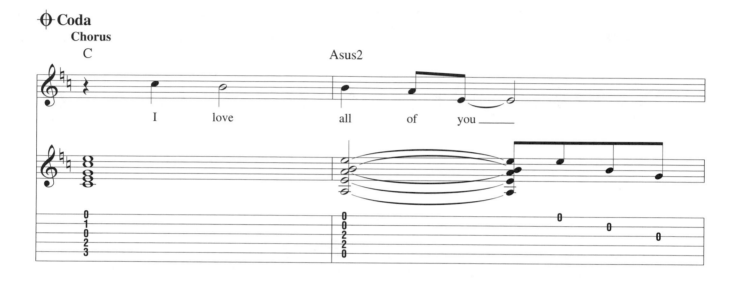

## Outro

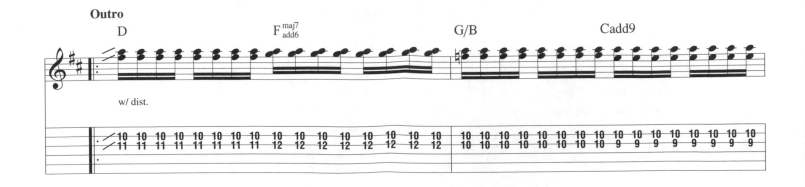

w/ dist.

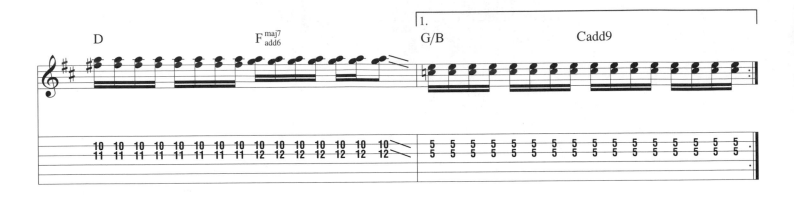

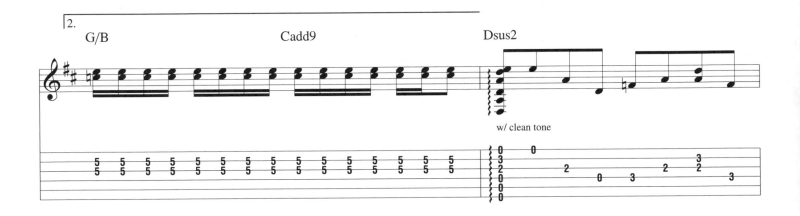

w/ clean tone

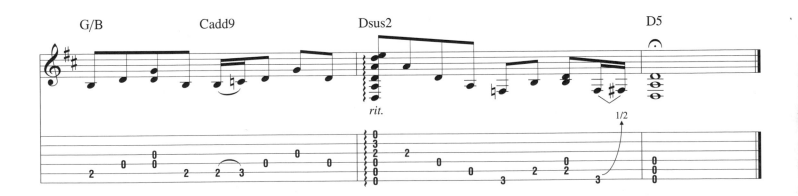

rit.

*Additional Lyrics*

4. I heard a little girl and what she said was something beautiful.
   To give your love no matter what is what she said.

# Name

**Words and Music by John Rzeznik**

Tuning:
(low to high) D-A-↑E-↑A-↑E-E

**Intro**
**Moderately fast** ♩ = 148
**Half-time feel**

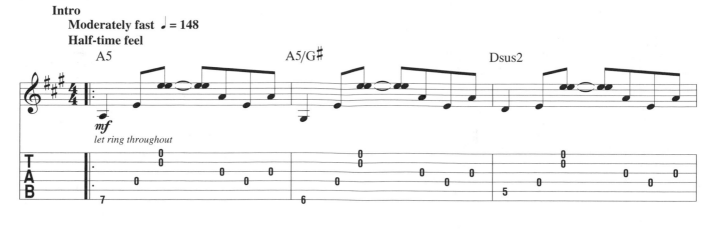

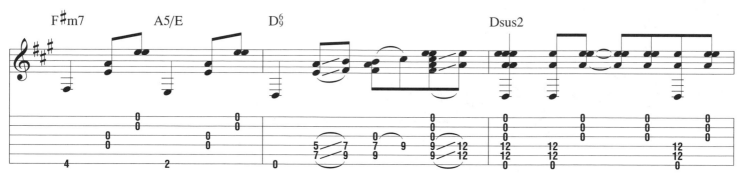

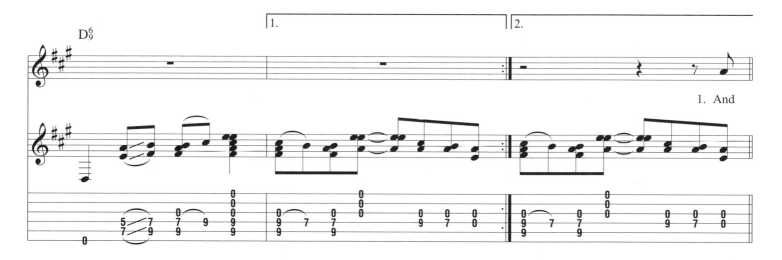

1. And

**Verse**

e - ven though __ the mo - ment passed __ me by, ____ I
2. *See additional lyrics*

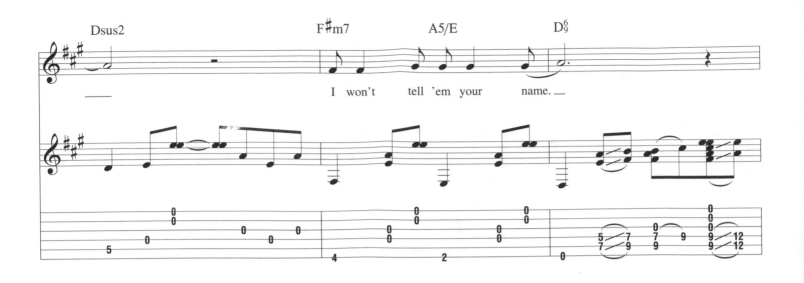

I won't tell 'em your name. —

**End half-time feel**

Ow!

**Guitar Solo**

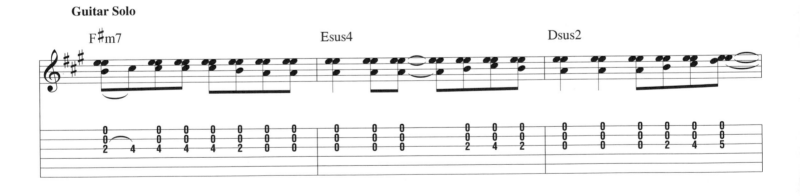

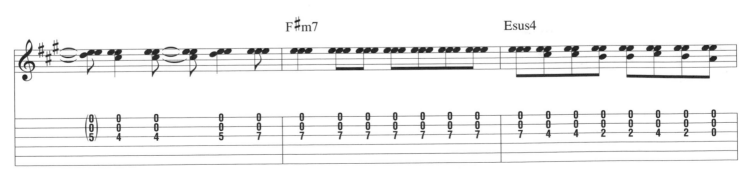

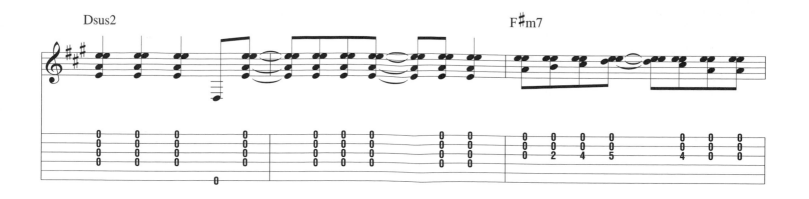

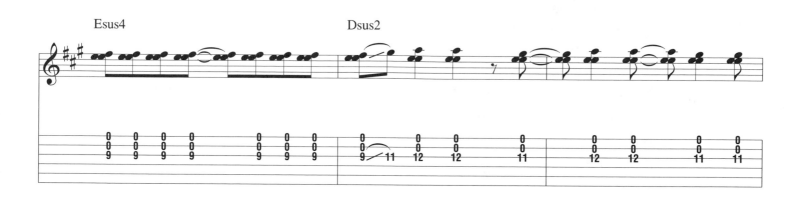

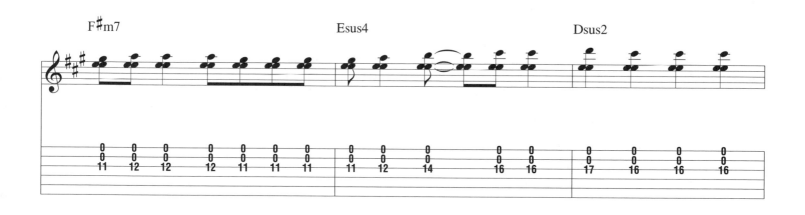

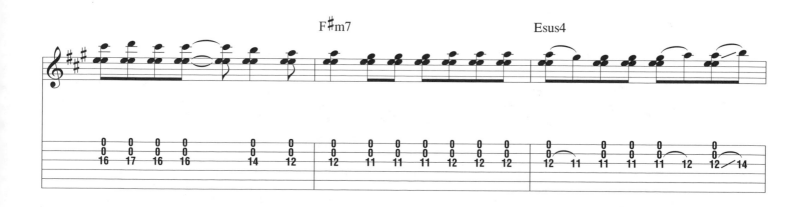

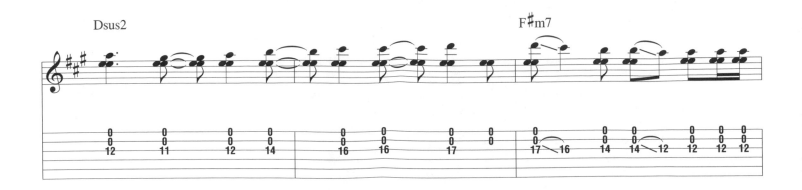

### Verse
**Half-time feel**

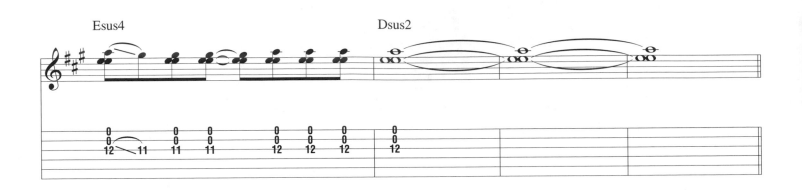

3. I think a-bout ___ you all ___ the time, ___ but

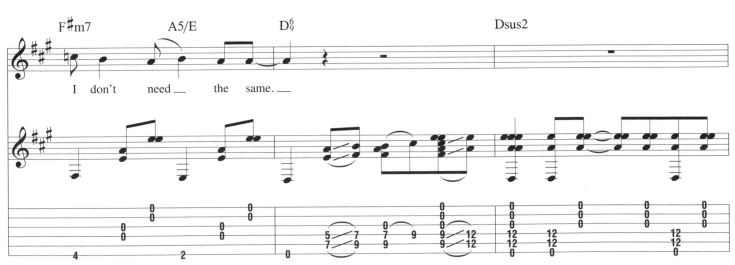

I don't need ___ the same. ___

It's lone-ly where ___ you are. ___

___ Come ___ back down ___ and I won't tell 'em your ___ name. ___

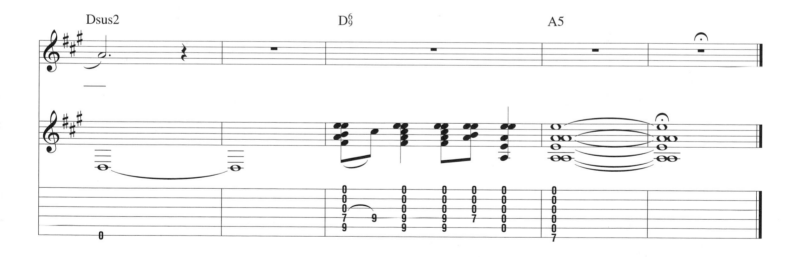

*Additional Lyrics*

2. Scars are souvenirs you never lose;
   The past is never far.
   And did you lose yourself somewhere out there?
   Did you get to be a star?
   And don't it make you sad to know that life
   Is more than who we are?

*Chorus*  We grew up way too fast,
   Now there's nothin' to believe,
   And reruns all become our history.
   A tired song keeps playin' on a tired radio.
   And I won't tell no one your name,
   And I won't tell 'em your name.

# What I Got (Reprise)

Words and Music by Brad Nowell and Lindon Roberts

**Verse**

1. Ear - ly in the morn - in', ris - in' to the street.

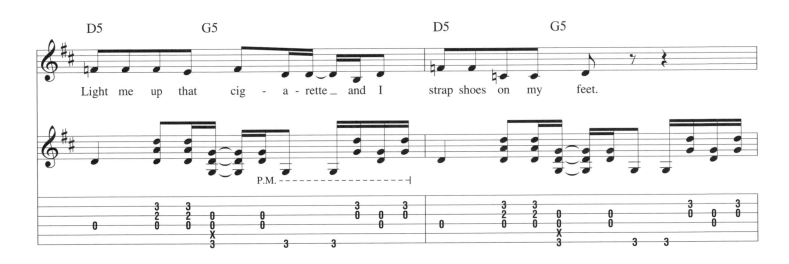

Light me up that cig - a - rette _ and I strap shoes on my feet.

Got to find a rea - son, rea - son things _ went wrong. _

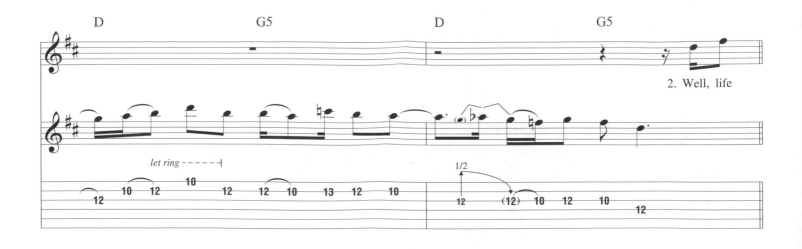

2. Well, life

**Verse**

is too short, so love __ the one you got 'cause you might get run o - ver or you might get shot.

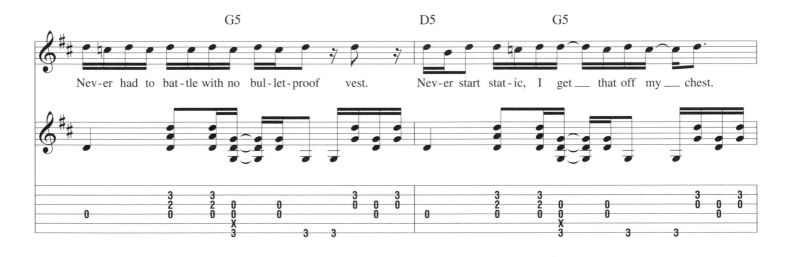

Nev-er had to bat-tle with no bul-let-proof vest. Nev-er start stat-ic, I get __ that off my __ chest.

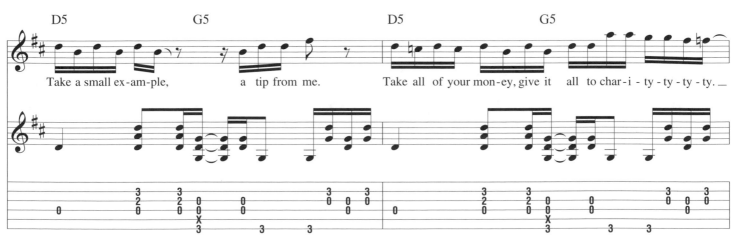

Take a small ex-am-ple, a tip from me. Take all of your mon-ey, give it all to char-i - ty - ty - ty - ty. __

Lov - in' ___ is what I got. ___ I said re - mem - ber that. ___

let ring - - - - -

**Interlude**

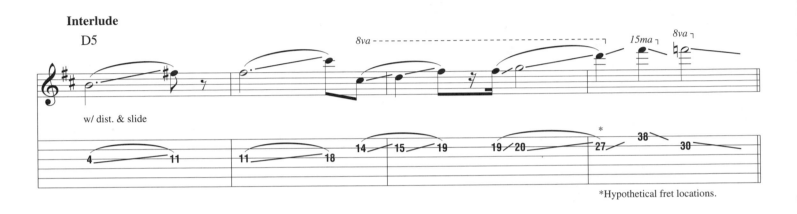

w/ dist. & slide

*Hypothetical fret locations.

**Verse**

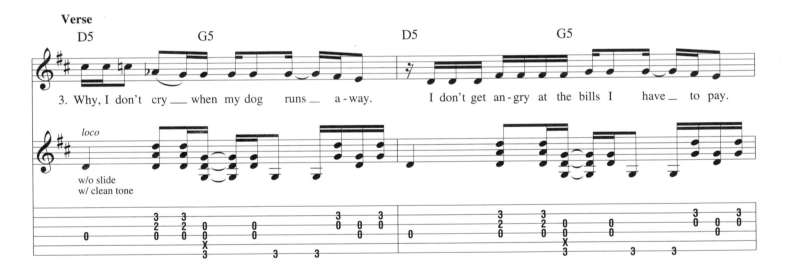

3. Why, I don't cry ___ when my dog runs ___ a - way. I don't get an - gry at the bills I have ___ to pay.

loco

w/o slide
w/ clean tone

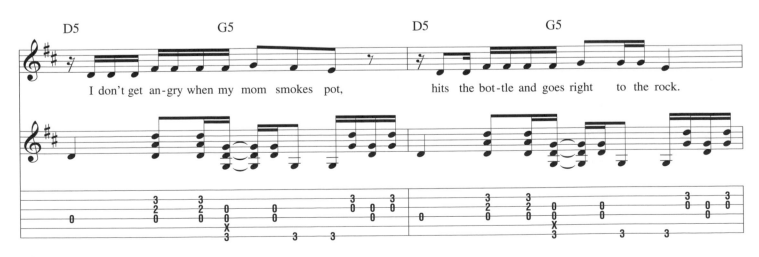

I don't get an - gry when my mom smokes pot, hits the bot - tle and goes right to the rock.

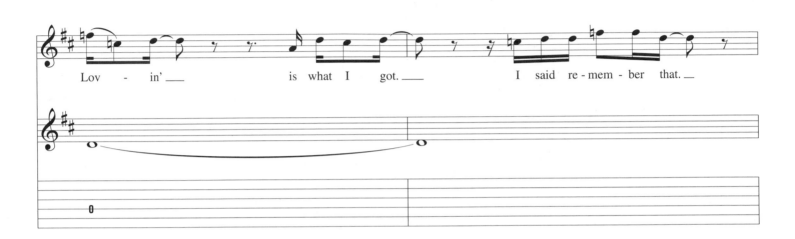

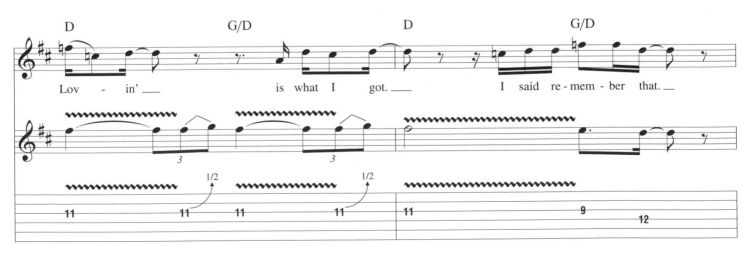

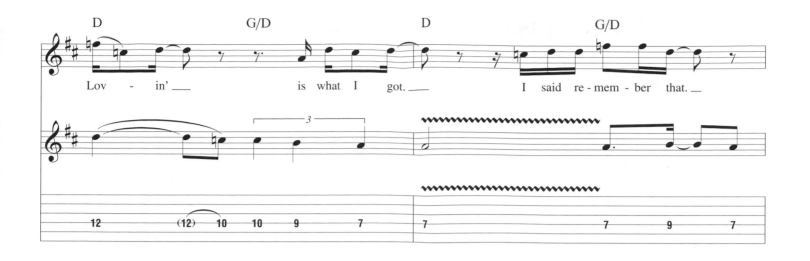

Lov - in' ___ is what I got. ___ I said re - mem - ber that. ___

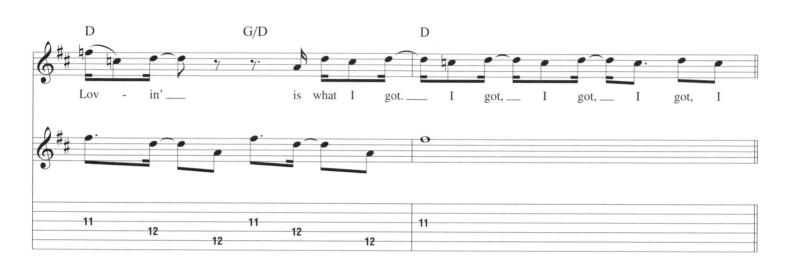

Lov - in' ___ is what I got. ___ I got, ___ I got, ___ I got, I

**Outro**

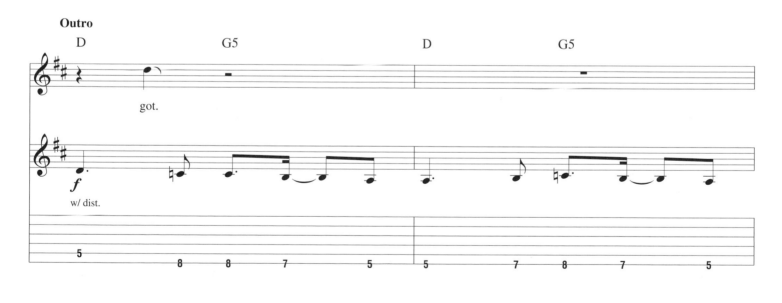

got.

w/ dist.

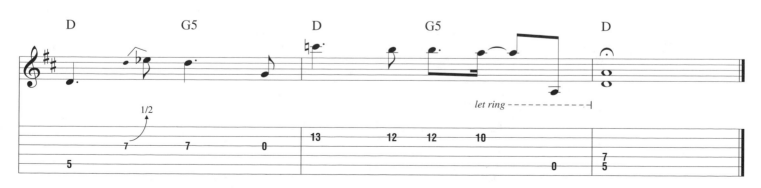

let ring - - - - - - - - - -

# The World I Know

Words and Music by Ed Roland and Ross Brian Childress

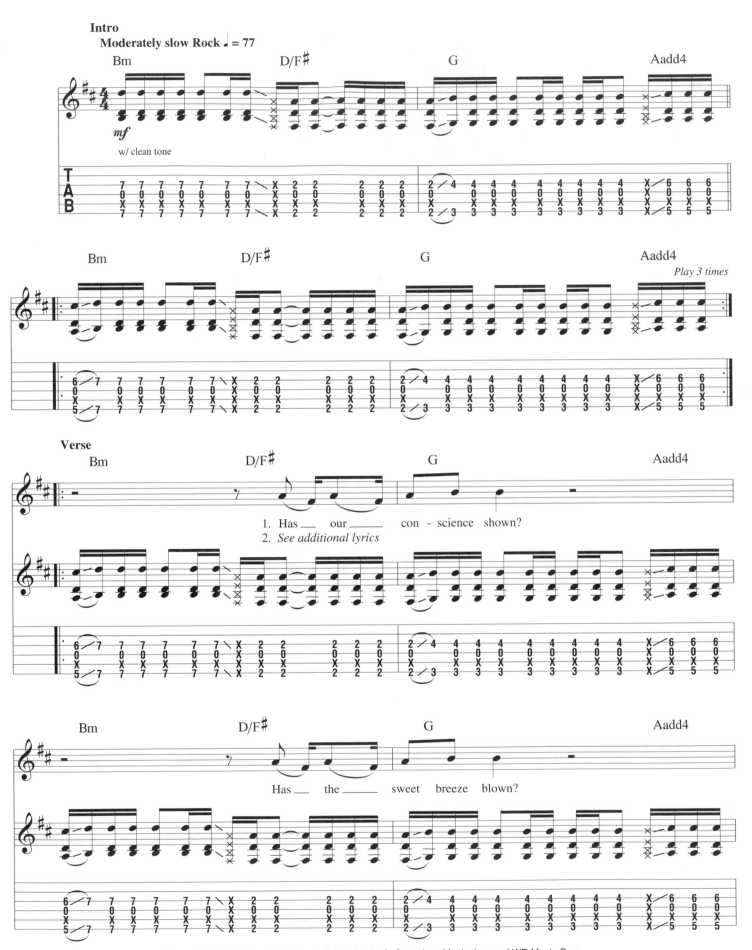

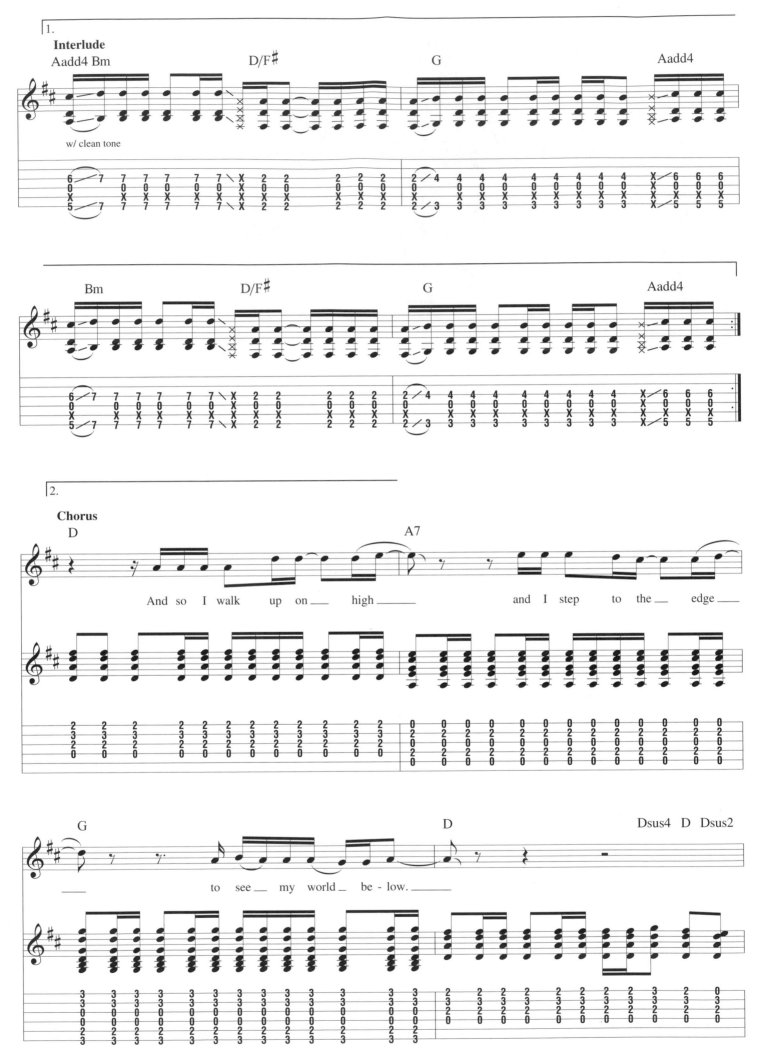

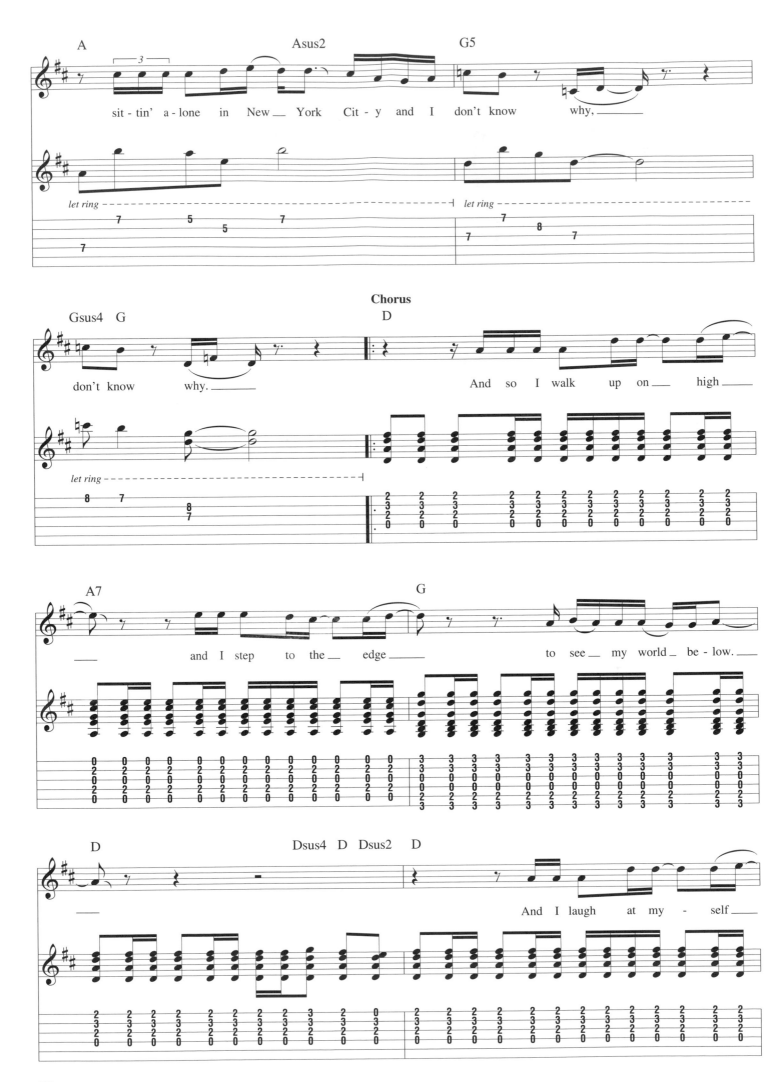

*Additional Lyrics*

2. Are we listening?
   Hymns of offering.
   Have we eyes to see
   Love is gathering?

*Pre-Chorus 2.* All the words that I've been reading
   Have now started the act of bleeding into one, into one.

# HAL·LEONARD GUITAR PLAY·ALONG®

This series will help you play your favorite songs quickly and easily. **INCLUDES TAB** Just follow the tab and listen to the CD to hear how the guitar should sound, and then play along using the separate backing tracks. Mac or PC users can also slow down the tempo without changing pitch by using the CD in their computer. The melody and lyrics are included in the book so that you can sing or simply follow along.

*Prices, contents, and availability subject to change without notice.*

FOR MORE INFORMATION, SEE YOUR LOCAL MUSIC DEALER,
OR WRITE TO:

## HAL·LEONARD® CORPORATION
7777 W. BLUEMOUND RD. P.O. BOX 13819 MILWAUKEE, WI 53213

**Visit Hal Leonard online at www.halleonard.com**

**Complete song lists available online.**

0308